PowerKiDS Readers

AMERICAN SYMBOLS
SÍMBOLOS DE AMÉRICA

THE WHITE HOUSE
LA CASA BLANCA

Joe Gaspar
Traducción al español: Eduardo Alamán

PowerKiDS press

New York

Published in 2014 by The Rosen Publishing Group, Inc.
29 East 21st Street, New York, NY 10010

First Edition

Editor: Amelie von Zumbusch
Book Design: Colleen Bialecki

Traducción al español: Eduardo Alamán

Photo Credits: Cover jiawangkun/Shutterstock.com; p. 5 Kamil Macniak/Shutterstock.com; p. 7 Handout/Getty Images; p. 9 Stock Montage/Archive Photos/Getty Images; pp. 11, 23 iStockphoto/Thinkstock; p. 13 Panoramic Images/Getty Images; p. 15 Chip Somodevilla/Getty Images; p. 17 Barry Winiker/Photolibrary/Getty Images; p. 19 fotosearch/stringer/Archive Photos/Getty Images; p. 21 Mandel Ngan/AFP/Getty Images.

Library of Congress Cataloging-in-Publication Data

Gaspar, Joe.
 The White House = La Casa Blanca / by Joe Gaspar ; translated by Eduardo Alamán. — First edition.
    pages cm. — (Powerkids readers: American symbols = Símbolos de América)
 English and Spanish.
 Includes index.
 ISBN 978-1-4777-1206-1 (library binding)
 1. White House (Washington, D.C.)—Juvenile literature. 2. Washington (D.C.)—Buildings, structures, etc.—Juvenile literature. I. Alamán, Eduardo translator. II. Gaspar, Joe. White House. III. Gaspar, Joe. White House. Spanish. IV. Title. V. Title: Casa Blanca.
 F204.W5G3718 2014
 975.3—dc23
                                2012046767

Web Sites: Due to the changing nature of Internet links, PowerKids Press has developed an online list of Web sites related to the subject of this book. This site is updated regularly. Please use this link to access the list: www.powerkidslinks.com/pkras/house/

Manufactured in the United States of America

CPSIA Compliance Information: Batch #S13PK4: For Further Information contact Rosen Publishing, New York, New York at 1-800-237-9932

CONTENTS

CONTENIDO

This is the **White House**.

Esta es la **Casa Blanca**.

U.S. **presidents** live there.

En la Casa Blanca viven los **presidentes** de los Estados Unidos.

John Adams was the first
one to live there.

John Adams fue el primer
presidente que vivió en la
Casa Blanca.

It is at 1600 Pennsylvania Avenue.

La Casa Blanca se encuentra en el 1600 de la Avenida Pensilvania.

James Hoban designed it.

Fue diseñada por
James Hoban.

It is big.

_____

Es una casa grande.

It has 132 rooms.

Tiene 132 habitaciones.

Running water was added in 1833.

_____

En 1833 se le dio agua corriente.

It has many **gardens**.

Tiene muchos **jardines**.

You can visit it!

¡Tú puedes visitar la
Casa Blanca!

WORDS TO KNOW/
PALABRAS QUE DEBES SABER

garden
(el) jardín

president
(el) presidente

White House
(la) Casa Blanca

INDEX

ÍNDICE